RIFT OF LIGHT

RIFT OF LIGHT

WILLIAM LOGAN

PENGUIN POETS

PENGUIN BOOKS

An imprint of Penguin Random House LLC
375 Hudson Street
New York, New York 10014
penguin.com

LIBRARY OF CONGRESS CATALOGING-IN-PUBLICATION DATA
Names: Logan, William, 1950 November 16- author.
Title: Rift of light / William Logan.
Description: New York, New York : Penguin Books, [2017] |
Series: Penguin poets
Identifiers: LCCN 2017007683 | ISBN 9780143131823 (paperback)
Subjects: | BISAC: POETRY / American / General.
Classification: LCC PS3562.O449 A6 2017 | DDC 811/.54—dc23
LC record available at https://lccn.loc.gov/2017007683

Printed in the United States of America

1 3 5 7 9 10 8 6 4 2

Set in Bembo Std
Designed by Ginger Legato

for Jamie Fellner and Karen Jardim

CONTENTS

II

III

IV

ACKNOWLEDGMENTS

Battersea Review: After Eden; A Cloudy Sunset in East Anglia; The Midwife Toad. *Birmingham Poetry Review*: Bad Garden; Descending into Philadelphia. *Blackbird*: Sincerity. *Boulevard*: Fall in the Sketch Pad; Venice in Rough Light. *Carolina Quarterly*: On the Consolations of Faith. *Cincinnati Review*: The Needle. *Compose*: The Locked Closet; The Other Other Country. *Hopkins Review*: The Kiss; Winter in Cloud; Sunday Out. *Hudson Review*: The Pheasant in His Empires. *Journal*: Winter Before Winter. *Journal of Florida Studies*: The Retention Pond. *Life and Legends*: Moth. *Nation*: Snow. *New Criterion*: The Harbor; Leaf Color; Mug Shot; The Venetian Dog. *New England Review*: Bruno; Long Island. Summer. 1968.; On the Late Latin Light; Venice in the Ordinary. *New Republic*: Sea Turtles. *New York Sun*: The Mail. *New Yorker*: Mysteries of the Armchair. *Notre Dame Review*: The Clipper Ships; The Servants' Stairs; Then, in the Trumpetings. *Parnassus*: There

Was; Lt. Selkirk on the *Weymouth*. *Pleiades*: Melville in the Straits; Midges in Material Form. *Plume* (online): Night World; On the Banks of the Allegheny; The Other Life. *PN Review*: The Field. *Poem-a-Day* (online): Complaint. *Poetry*: The Box Kite; Christmas Trees; In the Gallery of the Ordinary; Thoreau. *Poetry Northwest*: On Reading That the Ozone Is in Danger from Air Conditioning and Amphibious Life from Shampoo. *Raritan*: My Grandfather's Second Wife to My Father, 1958; The Troubles. *Salmagundi*: Martin Luther, 1525. *Sewanee Review*: Sonnet. *Sewanee Theological Review*: Dürer's Stag Beetle. *Smartish Pace*: The War. *Southwest Review*: The End of the Road. *32 Poems*: Venice in the Old Days. *TLS*: In the Dedication Lay the Index; The Landscape as Holy Order; Louise Brooks; On Hair as a Revolutionary Mode of Dress. *Two Bridges Review*: In Medias Res; Little Compton; The Storm. *Virginia Quarterly Review*: A Garret in Paris; To a Former Beauty. *Warwick Review*: Mary Sowle. *Yale Review*: The Abandoned Crow; Clouds; My Father in the Shadows.

RIFT OF LIGHT

A couple of hours I had noticed a growing rift of light in the clouds to the west; it looked as if the dull day might have a rich ending.

—George Gissing, *New Grub Street*

Here and there a little smooth water, an occasional rift of light through the clouds—alas! only to be followed by greater darkness.

—William Ingraham Russell, *The Romance and Tragedy of a Widely Known Business Man of New York*

I

Thoreau

That oily bale of rags, lost'
to the silent architectures of the wood—
or so it seemed, as the fall's chancels
darkened, and rough earth gave and forgave.
Forgave, I mean, the intrusion.

Leaf Color

A steely torn silver, rusted along the edges;
the faint acidic yellow, like the backwash
of a polluted pond; earth-spatter

and gold spot in blotchy shallows;
grays the purpling of drenched slate;
and a pooling crimson with the false

bonhomie of the maraschino cherry—
all that unnecessary life turning to tinder.
The shadows were fragile-fertile

beyond the shocks of grimy hay in a spent field.
The India-ink, closeted blacks—
why choose the easeful darks?

Not that anything lay hidden there.
Was it only the spilled-over, abandoned life
and, from the wastage, the broken buds?

On the Late Latin Light

The semiprecious sunset, windswept, vain,
took the cold buttery light and made it work.
Myopia blurred the rain, laying the dust.
It was elegiac lite, in other words.
The window framed a gallery of garden,
wisteria draped along the mossy fence,
the lilac punk-show of a woodblock print,
as if a chisel could engrave a thought.
There was an hour when style was not the cause.
Jerome in his ink-blotched study, lion and skull
props in some fantasy of scholarship,
scratched down the words of God in his own tongue.
Latin was not the tongue, I forgot to add.
He was the odd man out, or in, perhaps.

Martin Luther, 1525

Old Cranach's Luther, Protestant sincerity
dissolved in paint. The boy monk's inkblot cloak
swallows him like a python taking a goat,
the dull face slope-jawed, bangs unbarbered, long
longing for the tincture of the cell.
The brute uncertain jowls below his stare
complain, *What I have seen, I have not seen.*
Struck by a bolt on the Cunard Line to Patmos,
he hung his theses on a marlinspike
the iron of oxidizing heretics,
his Christ the jailer-headsman of new souls.
Said, *We are beggars*, by way of epitaph,
not a bad way to end, or to begin.
I honor him, he who stayed petulant, blastproof.

Bad Garden

During the time of the Tulipomania, a speculator
often offered and paid large sums for a root which he
never received and never wished to receive.
—Johann Beckmann, *A History of Inventions and Discoveries*

Spattered with indigo,
the prickly borage
conquers the roses
like a Mongol horde—

not the lancers
of the Great Khan, perhaps,
but unshaven bankers
intent on a hostile takeover.

Tulips were big money in 1637,
when a Dutchman
could swap his brewery
for a rare bulb—but not

such sullen, go-ahead
Wall Streeters, hedge funds
hardly worth plucking for a salad.
Are such petite

flowers devious, coquettish but shy,
waiting until your back is turned
to blossom, or wilt,
or contract some unsightly disease,

a reminder of secret ecstasies
and conjoined humiliations?
Perhaps they are as much
as we shall ever know

of the beautiful.

Bruno

A nerveless pigeon perches, triumphant,
upon your bronze head. However artless
the interrogators with their docket of charges,

however apologetic the torturers with their brands,
you survive the acids of history.
The clerks of submission lie almost at peace.

Platonic Rome—that hotbed of democracies,
the cant of lecture—worries into the new century,
as if on a shopping tour. In the whirl of traffic

beyond Trajan's Column, in the hieroglyphs
of the signboard and politician's bill,
lies the palazzo of memory, its gilt couches

and spindly armchairs burning with remonstrance
like the leftovers of a yard sale. The lost canals
claim their unquiet rest. Bruno, the Campo

de' Fiori would be empty now, but for your ash.

Clouds

By night, tarnished silver
whipped past on west winds, hurrying

after some unmet appointment,
dark and quarrelsome, or given to tears.

They passed in ranked orders, the clouds,
as the first blackbird aria broke,

hoarse practice for the racket to come.
That morning, they resembled nothing,

no Rorschach in the sky kept un-empty
for the theologies of vacancy.

One old master piled cotton wool on a table
and stared until he found the sky.

Later Gainsborough propped up sprigs
of broccoli for his far woods,

with stubs of moss for bushes,
and rocks of cork and coal.

The Clipper Ships

> True, I have follow'd the rough trade of war
> With some success, and can without a blush
> Review the shaken fort, and sanguine plain.
>
> —Edward Young, *Busiris*

Under bleached, burnt-out dawns,
the loblollies cut the crystalline fog

like masts. Enter the magnolias,
puffy blossoms yellowed as old china plates,

with much to teach us about rough trade.

In Medias Res

> The whale looked like a portly burgher smoking his
> pipe of a warm afternoon.
>
> —Melville, *Moby-Dick*

We woke to the advertisement for our lives.
Heat withered the air in the listed flat
with its horizontal slit-windows.
We looked at nature through a turret.
The ceiling had begun to turn to salt.

The Landscape as Holy Order

> The marks [that the sharks] thus leave on the whale,
> may best be likened to the hollow made by a carpenter
> in countersinking for a screw.
>
> —Melville, *Moby-Dick*

Dusty cow-parsley, red slash of poppies,
crushed gather of hedges rimed with snow-blossom,
these, these too, abide in the faint election
of those reserved, reserving appetites.

Why go over what has gone before—
pilgrims of correction, even the static century
in which nothing yet has happened?
Beyond, after all, lie the seas

where fins steeple the dark, moving in for the kill.

The Abandoned Crow

With cocked head,
it raked the ground
under one anthracite eye,

a shadow in shadow.
The crow sidled the railing
and stopped

to review, like Kant,
the villainies of the aesthetic.
The gardens had grown

to weeds, the weeds
to briars. It pecked
the black cloth of a book.

It slipped a tarnished coin
into its beak.
Ragged at the ends,

its wings wore
the sheen of watered silk.
The crow flew into the gutter

to consider the ideas of order,
or a rusty piece of wire
twisted like a spiral staircase.

Fall in the Sketch Pad

That mortal man should feed upon the creature that
feeds his lamp, and . . . eat him by his own light, as
you may say; this seems so outlandish a thing.

—Melville, *Moby-Dick*

The gray damage hung over the roof tiles,
that late light passing for annunciation.
They were almost our fathers, the headless statues
lagged in their rows down the dead garden.

Then the streetlamps died, as if soon
it would be dawn. A scatter of pink petals
dampened the walk, the petals too like your flesh,
that shocking warmth beneath.

The Needle

The traveller who at the present day is content to
travel in the good old Asiatic style . . . will find ample
food for poetic reflection in the singular scenery.

—Melville, *Israel Potter*

Oh, the usual derangement of yew trees
rising over the garden wall like Japanese mountains.
Teacups of roses like drops of blood.
The lichen-measled walk. A sharp sun,

wary as the light in de la Tour.
Then age edged from the shadows,
the way paper rots from the margin.
On that ferry to Dover,

your half-closed eye disclosed its darkness,
the eye of a needle.
After those words unsaid,
the sky pumped full of preposterous dye.

Complaint

The faucets squeeze
out a dribble of rust.
The stained slipcovers

fray like sea wrack. Scruffy, haggled
weeds jailed in broken pots;
shy, disfigured poppies;

a barked rose succumbing
to white-frocked aphids—
the garden doesn't work. The heater

doesn't work. Nothing works.
Who lives in such a house?
The pipes piss and moan,

as if forced to pay taxes.
If there are dream houses,
are there undreamed houses

full of the things we desire,
or only those we deserve?
Perhaps they are the homes

of strange gods with some
incomprehensible, whimsical
way of looking at things.

You said we waded through the mysteries to get here.

Midges in Material Form

A cloud blurs the wicker fence,
a stain where thistles starve the summer air,
the lilac shavings dropping as if burnt
onto the stone. That is the cost of refusal.
The speared wisteria, stiff, Japanese,
holds off the light, uneven in this season—
blunted, familiar, valedictory.
The early artists of wash, of body color,
stole the cold secrets of transparency.
They licked the brush and *there*, they stuck a tree,
a smudge the eye refused to call a birch.
Painting is still the material form of desire.
Unshaven sixty stares me in the face.
I cannot look at paint and not see death.

The Retention Pond

Thanksgiving's blanched happiness
come round again, the wood storks
hunch like Troy's elders along the wall,
uttering not a word of complaint.

In stoic progress they soldier on,
clerkishly planting one foot in the mud,
then another, opening a sheltering wing
as if by noblesse oblige. They eye each other

with respect—or is that suspicion?
The gray waters slick with light,
like a slate countertop, each spindly reed
grazing its mirror-double. And there,

through the breaks, a black boar
snuffles in shadow, like a gorged piggy bank.
All lower nature aspires to the Catholic—
large families and no birth control.

On a rotting post, our local Tiresias,
the lone anhinga, dries outspread wings,
just an advertisement for Barclays.
The old Hohenzollerns, they'd seen it all before.

Venice in Rough Light

> Tooth-powder— Magnesia— Macassar Oil— Some
> Gunpowder from Manton's
>
> —Lord Byron's shopping list, 1819

The brute city, perpendicular in cold,
welcomed us back like an old enemy.

The purples slouched behind the terra-cotta,
a thin light stalking limestone parapets,
glinting off capstones, worming the old scars.
Snow pelted down like specks of Styrofoam,
the gutters filling with torn envelopes
or sugar dumped on ruined documents.

Emptiness shivered along the palazzo
shuttered or abandoned, dried lemon flaking the
    walls.
Upright, as if from Darwin's illustrations,
the model ghosts walked backward to the sea.
You turned to me then, turned for the first time.

II

In the Dedication Lay the Index

June.
The silent heats,
and those not silent: bird-
cry, the bloated moan of cattle,
the lonely, repetitive wail of the car alarm.

Long Island. Summer. 1968.

after Thomas Jones, *Rooftops in Naples*

Beneath that chalk-blue sky with iron
stirred through it, the whitewashed windows
burned in faint phosphorescence. That long forgotten
summer, amid the ghostly Long Island yachts,
we entered the waters on that narrow neck
beneath a moon of cracked porcelain.
Our blank lives had almost begun.
War rose behind the shuttered summer, that summer.
We whispered beneath low masses
of anchored boats, stirring through that coldness,
the phosphor radiant along bodies
naked in their nakedness. There in the iced waters,
our glowing outlines almost made us whole.

Mug Shot

Los Angeles

Almost nineteen, with Rita Hayworth hair,
lips parted in the sorrow of seduction,
she has arrowed on thin eyebrows.

Her name, according to the mug shot,
is Ernesteen, though beneath it
someone has penciled *Delores.*

She might not have chosen to wear this,
her department-store blouse, ruched at the neck,
showing off the sculptural lines of a face

that must have drawn attention
even from strangers.
Perhaps that was the problem.

She looks like a woman caught
somewhere she shouldn't have been.
It was 1950, after all, and a narcotics bust

was something to think about,
even if you were white, and pretty,
and thought you knew your way around.

Must I mention that she is beautiful,
this Renaissance face caught with a look of surprise
by the flash of the police photographer?

On the Consolations of Faith

The day a steam bath, all life mildewed in incident.
Ahead lay the raw-gated city, at ease
as a retired banker in a chaise longue,
or the murderer who dies unrepentant.

The train took its time, the rural out of date.
Time raked the worm from the soil,
eased the nighthawk from the civic trees.
The reach of yellow field, just out of reach,

promised an abundance that falls from faith,
where hedges break a communion of berry
and dry channels stir the wounded stream
waiting for Advent to come round again.

The Kiss

When I hear of Schrödinger's cat, I reach for my pistol.

—Stephen Hawking

Moody, jet-haired, she was a whole philosophy—
just another girl, perhaps, but not to me.

When she kissed me roughly on the lips,
as if I'd been staggered by two battleships,

I lay on the cooling sand,
my old life a conjunction—*and*,

or *or*, perhaps, or *yet*. Or *but*.
I touched my mouth, bleeding from an invisible cut.

And that was all. One kiss by the glaring bay—
sometimes love happens that way.

A few nights later, this local goddess turned
and said carelessly, in a way that burned,

"I've never thought of you that way, I guess."
She touched me then with the ghost of a caress.

Now, when we happen to meet,
a wall of glass rises on the street

or in the bar where we've gone for a drink,
she grabbing in her purse, the night again like ink.

Some know who they are by what is missing.
Perhaps there's a world where we kept kissing,

where we married, had three kids,
and did what decency now forbids.

Nothing terrible happened, no one was swept away,
and our lives continued almost the same way.

The Harbor

The tiresome *creak* of the harbor—
fishing sloops at anchor, trying their lines,

and the crestfallen wharf building, clapboards
scoured of their last drip of paint.

The tin sinks, bigger than horse tubs,
groaned with senatorial lobsters

and rude spitting steamers.
Perhaps just the bridge on its last legs,

or piers, rather, shifting over the tidal river
that never changed its mood for the better.

Of a Sunday, when sailboats tilted
toward the river mouth—Cuttyhunk

and Martha's Vineyard beyond—
someone unseen cranked open the bridge,

using a complicated system of gears
that required an hour of fuss.

The Packards and Fords backed up
along the approach strewn with oyster-shells,

the cars filled with quarrelsome children,
mothers fanning themselves with a sandy catalogue,

and fathers thumbing the cellophane
from a new pack of Lucky Strikes or Camels,

wheeling the smoke out cranked-down windows
as if they had all the time in the world.

"One day, *we'll* sail there," my father said.

Sincerity

All sympathy not consistent with acknowledged virtue
is but disguised selfishness.

—Coleridge, *The Table Talk and Omniana*

That word again, haunting Coleridge
like a hellhound, rolling like a dislodged boulder.

I mean, crushing all.
There was perhaps sincerity in the kingfisher

perched on the concrete edge
of the artificial pond, the reedy stalks

gray with frost, and distantly the *pluck-pluck*
of the local woodpecker. There was our furniture,

the sublime that remained slime,
the fluff-headed mergansers cruising still waters,

ever on the make. I saw everything,
I thought. Not the hours longing

for the blunt knife of her gaze. Not the haze
of philosophy, or *millefiori*, for that. Ah, ah.

Once the "silent majority" meant the dead.

The Storm

Rags of cloud east, in ordinary time,
brought down the chimney and burst the ancient window,
as if an elbow had gone through it.

The orchid sky feathered the gables,
and a last yellow leaf flagged on the evening
breezes. The lateen angle cut the dead housetops,
the shadow fierce and particular, like a wandering Jew.

It was a world of almost nothing, or almost of nothing.
A single star hung on the backdrop like an ornament.

Melville in the Straits

> For unless you own the whale, you are but a provincial and
> sentimentalist in Truth. But clear Truth is a thing for
> salamander giants only to encounter; how small the chances
> for the provincials then?
>
> —Melville, *Moby-Dick*

Dawn blazed the snuff-inked cloud, whose solemn glints
hinted at unseen gilt interiors
crackling across the bias of horizon,
the line of bearing the *Pequod* hammered home.
Home where the garden was blown with oak-shelled snails,
the morbid lilac flushed on pea-black stone,
the shadow world made justice for itself.
A man can lose his faith and still cheat God,
wetting the dried-up brush upon his tongue.
He scans the dead like a physiognomist,
a man-o'-war bird boiled in philosophy—
no hero promised, no chapter ever right
in which brute fate had happened, had to happen.
The ocean was his organized religion.

The Midwife Toad

> "You know the old man's ivory leg, well I dreamed
> he kicked me with it."
>
> —Melville, *Moby-Dick*

The maples blush in afterlight
under cold stars that boil the gables and slates.
The midwife toad tries out its telegraph.

Sing to me now, Old Wart, as if you owned
the disconnected alleys of your domain.
Newfangled exile without a proper visa,

who would be king but the discontented soul?

To a Former Beauty

You flared across Boston
like a meteor, blond mane and lowered brow
in every coffeehouse off the Charles.
I could tell your conquests

by their cancerous looks.
You were a Cato among novelists,
breaking a man because you could.
The glazes of the river stood in warning.

Now the wrinkles gather like suitors
along your lips, and there's a mothy flutter
beneath your left eye. Ah,
and that pressed-dough face, which once,

once, might have launched a thousand
slips of the tongue.

Venice in the Ordinary

> "You English intellectuals will be the death of us all."
> —*The Man Who Knew Too Much*

Off Leg-Break Alley, the white-aproned boy
applied gold leaf to a damaged angel,
wild-haired, staked down
for its beauty treatment. Tourists once more,

we were seeking the workshops of the fallen.
Even our conversations foundered
on the *déjà vu* of repetition. The spare trees
on the piazza, riffled by hot wind,

loosed the skirts of the Aegean. Wavelets
breached the staccato strokes of Canaletto,
dapper gray mustaches on pea-green swells,
marking the come-and-go of light. Habit

becomes the mother-monster of art.
I felt chilled, as if for a moment
I had seen my own gravestone. It was just
the boy, and the boyish angel carved

a century or two before, needing that renewal
of the skin, the fallen desire.

The Locked Closet

Being clothed we shall not be found naked.

—2 Corinthians

In shadowed ranks, the suitcases huddled,
dozens of them—rusty leather satchels, alligator grips,

Gladstone bags with worn labels of European hotels.
Some of the cases had burst open, exhausted by the wait.

Others had been forced to yield their secrets, disgorging
flowered tea-dresses of some long-forgotten fashion,

collarless shirts in fading antique stripes.
A dozen hats slumped half naked in blown carrying-cases.

And shoes! There lay a rat's nest of brogues and oxfords,
even a hobnail Abraham Lincoln might have worn!

The abandoned clothes suffered like good servants,
still patient for their masters. It was only an obscure

New England town, but once the Magi
had left their luggage behind, intending to return.

After Eden

Before us lay mud–bestrewn banks,
the flats rutted and torn,

as if cast from molds already broken.
The Lazarus ridges were picked out in pine,

the sun, those silent hours, barely rising
above the eastern mountains.

I had imagined something different,
those days I thought about the future.

You looked older,
the hard lines scoured into your face.

Long afternoons upon the piazza,
we sipped some Venetian variant of coffee,

the richer for being thick with the sediment
of Byzantium. The Arsenale stood empty of keels,

the mazy canals mossy with trash.
We were young then. So there we waited,

having made a small mistake involving the fruit,
or the fruit salad, condemned to the view,

if it could be called a view, of hills bare
as a scalp, nothing upon their nakedness

but some Platonic idea of vacancy.
This is heaven, you said.

Someday you should get a look at hell.

A Garret in Paris

If you leaned over
the peeling window ledge,
one tower of Notre Dame
rose over a rusty bridge.

The puckered Seine labored
down to the storm-tossed coast
while you sat smiling
above the burnt toast.

Each morning your new face
stood modeled in the light,
holding back the feeling
never allowed to ignite.

Darkly underground,
the Métro rumbled on.
You lifted a black eyebrow.
Something there was gone,

and in the air grew
the feathery sound of wings,
like an Annunciation,
among other things.

Moth

Green of old jade, trim as a Tiffany brooch
against the breech of clapboard

in the hard light of noon, the dust moth
was a leftover of the other world—

lost, abandoned, perhaps mislaid,
or found at some inconvenient hour,

like an umbrella after a spring shower.

III

Little Compton

Young Doctor von Trapp
of the singing von Trapps
aimed at my knee with the reflex hammer,
its rubber head a pink triangle of gum.
The leg leapt forward on its own.
They also called it a tomahawk hammer.

My Father in the Shadows

Mute in drink,
my father scraped a fork across the dinner plate.
Vermouth slouched in the cabinet.
The rotting Morgan had been auctioned off.

Bills layered his desk
like drafts of snow.
The house on Private Road in escrow,
its blowsy, prize-winning horse chestnut

cast off dandruff blossoms
that shrouded a swatch of lawn.
I've seen the satellite photo.
The new house verged on a ravine.

Something dead lay at the bottom.
The new kitchen was a galley
with a wobbly floor.
He had taken to pissing in crystal dinner-goblets.

Out the window,
the crocus's hairy eye
watched the snail-like progress of the snail,
but nothing stung him to words again.

There, on the desk, he had propped the Kodak
of my mother, feathered hat askew,
grinning like a demon
with a bald baby in her arms.

Mary Sowle

The butternut curl of honeysuckle spent
its somnolent perfumes.
Bees yellowed with pollen hung heavily
in summer's clotted air, when with our fellows

we gathered before the orb-weaver
to watch it do battle
with the Japanese beetle,
the first time I heard the phrase "Pyrrhic victory."

Was Mary Sowle
not unlike a spider, harboring the web
of some 1920s secret we were too young to know?
Only the memory, or half a memory,

of the graying brunette—bewigged?—
in that seaside village
troubles my recollection of the grass-verged macadam
that brought our houses formally together,

hers Gothic and in need of paint.
Down the road, the Methodists plied their trade
on bended knee, harmonizing to the blue firmament
I recognize now as populated with judgment.

The vanity of it! Those accusing looks!

The Mail

The cock's tail, cocked up, enameled—
so, the red flag on the steel mailbox
standing sentry by our stone wall,

the mail waiting to be pulled out
like an egg! Ah, wrong. Neighbors kept hens;
we waited for bills. Father had taken

to country ways, the gentleman
farmer with his one vacant field,
mown every year on Labor Day.

Who was he then, ten years home
from a war on the U.S.S.
Something-or-Other? Why not hole up

far from the head office
in a fishing village where every farm
had been seeded with arrowheads,

home to some Tripp or Sowle
whose father's father's father
lay in his grave

beside his father's father's father's father?
The town's two-room schoolhouse
had a witch for a principal,

a kindly witch; and one of the Sowles
swept it out every afternoon,
lining up oak desks as if with a ruler.

I was too young for a letter.
I watched the red cock's tail
with the patience of a hawk.

The Box Kite

The lift, the very lift and pull of it!
They'd wasted the summer morning,

father and son in the devil's
breath of July—gnats wheedling

madly above the drive—pasting Sunday comics
across the struts, like the canvas skin

of a Sopwith Camel. Into the close-gnawn yard
with its humpback boulder,

they dragged it triumphantly, unreeling the twine
until the contraption yanked itself

from bald earth, high above
the matchbox houses by the sweetly reeking bog,

beneath the shadow of woods,
to a height where a boy might peer over the horizon

to Boston—and beyond, the ocean.
The son was my father. I tottered at his legs,

having borrowed his name and my grandfather's.
They paid out the ramshackle affair

until it became a postage stamp. The line
burned a bloody groove into my palms,

the last time they stood at ease with each other.

On the Banks of the Allegheny

We had started over again—
an unpainted house with the new Chevy in the drive,

the model with the push-button transmission.
The lots were new. Rich brown

like expensive leather, the fresh turds
nested in the unseeded lawn,

shivering with inner life,
the maggots squirming wildly toward the light.

The Other Other Country

The days bled alabaster,
the nothing of sky over Paradise,

where the original sin was weather.
Did they miss the wildness

of the palms, the angels
who brought breakfast on tea trays?

Each dawn would be a palimpsest
of storms almost forgotten,

humiliation, love.

The Other Life

I possessed a secret life: the seedy coastal town,
the shuttered colonial of twining hallways,
a wife with the flaring prettiness
of my mother, a smudge-mouthed child or two.

Awake, I never thought of that other life.
The two existed in mutual ignorance,
until one night the rough fields
and the volatile scent of my wife—my *wife!*—

with her Liz Taylor grin, her shock
of blond hair, rose from the smell
of my real garden. Had I died in my sleep,
I might have woken to that new life,

ignorant of what I had lost,
if indeed anything had been lost—
like the phosphorescent wake
trailing a swimmer in the bay.

My secret left the faintest trace:
the Atlantic over the dunes,
the north flecked with the fall
that *is* fall. One day the dream was gone,

had been gone some months,
like a gas flame blown out.

Mysteries of the Armchair

News of the world lay in the rain.
Maple leaves fell, pre-foxed,
as if stored for decades on library shelves.
The horse chestnuts had been oiled,

their waxy polish glowing
like the Madonna in the Portuguese church
up the harbor. Immaculate, without sin,
by winter they burned with mildew.

His fedora and trench coat damp in the closet,
Father in his armchair with an icy dry-martini
quarreled with the rose-trellised wallpaper.
Mother stood locked in the kitchen—

the *terra cognita* of canned vegetables,
pearly slabs of swordfish, the heaving
paper sack in which two ill-tempered lobsters
brooded over their death sentence.

Sonnet

All is confusion. Much is understood,
lost in the fractured hour the freezing wind
took to its silences, as in a wood
where automatic birds live dumb and blind.

Where is the hardship in such holiness?
Like the idea of God, or just the soul,
the beatitude of things lives on unseen.
Where did she go, the girl in the see-through dress?

Her open blouse, her razor, her window screen—
those partial partial things that made us whole.

Descending into Philadelphia

The chalk fields hung,
new snow planing away
all but stick-like trees
that fringed the blistered

stone walls, fatally unbalanced,
and the worn-out hose of black river.
The sovereign touch—that, that
too, proved a short fuse.

They were just toys,
the first rates and tall ships.
Cod balls, the disillusions of wine—
such the bill of fare

laid by, the iron beams
underpinning the Quaker
easements of conscience.
The plain man constitutes

my argument with history.
The Schuylkill lost its flocks
of mournful birds feeding
on politics, its "pontifical works."

In the Gallery of the Ordinary

In their excess, their blowsy dreaming
and King Solomon–like tempers, the clouds
possessed the grandeur of eighteenth-century oils,

when a painter earned his profession
as an anatomist. Those artists of verdigris
and gamboge, too gorged on joy, perhaps,

treated that blank pasture of the "heavens"
like something that had lived.
Their crawly undoings remind us

of the mean curiosities of sheep, the sea's
half-remembered boil, or a few twisted bolls
of cotton—the morning phosphorescent

or sunset a dull, worn-out gilt.
The nights there were scumbled with light.
How could we ever have taken them

for the abstinence of art?

Sunday Out

The rain day's a muddy blur in the foreground,
a John Crome elbowed into color,

frayed at the edges. The sublime rests like laid paper.
The lawns as well. The hours are translucent,

truculent, slipped onto the day's page
like the thinnest washes. Nature is the one thing

the Christian surrenders to the Lucretian.

The Field

The field was more a painting than a field,
the flowers oily in their despairing freshness

and, beyond, the scumble of jack pines,
the thumbed portion of stream. Along the stone wall,

a child's version of a wall, shocks of knee-grass
rose like lightning. We might have lived

in some summer-watercolorist's summer,
the afternoon like other afternoons

gathering in that field, arguing with that sky,
as if there were nothing to be done.

Sea Turtles

And there they were, sandy, armored,
clawing their way from beach potholes,

one with a fragment of egg stuck to his head.
The ocean lay exhausted,

a blue sheet feathered with froth,
working its businesslike way toward the dunes,

as if it had an appointment never to be met.
Baby waves fanned across the sand,

touched in by a painter in eyelash-dashes—
frayed and silvery. How damp and glittery

they looked, the sea turtles! They tumbled forth,
jerky as Chaplin or Harold Lloyd—

and stumped from step to step,
like rusty trucks bumping over a corduroy road.

On the horizon, the blot of a container ship
muscled along, running hours late,

or years, if it were owned by Zeno.
The sea lay always before them.

My Grandfather's Second Wife to My Father, 1958

Don, dearest,

      Please, please don't think ill of me.
I never wanted to break up our dear home,
   but I couldn't see
             the least turn for the better
             after all your father's "accidents."

      The poor guy will never change
so long as some floozie begs to be his crutch.
   All alcoholics
             hit bottom sooner or later.
             From there, they master it or perish.

      That dope just never wised up.
I feel a real heel being so tough on him.
   You tell me you think
             you got through to him. Hardy-har!
             Don't buy that stuff for a minute, Don.

      He'd promise you Red China
to get out of a jam. When a college man
   can't support himself,
             that's ridiculous, isn't it?
             Your dad goes about telling his pals

      I took him for every dime.
He spent everything he could draw, and then some.
   His bosses got smart—
             he never *ever* worked past noon,
            those months at Buffalo Electric.

No wonder you were so glad
to pull out of Cleveland. The further away
  you stay, the better.
          For God's sake, don't write him a word
      or you'll never get rid of the fool—

  that guy can be so darned sweet
when he needs to salve his poor wounded conscience.
  Send me a letter
        at my daughter's—the landlady
      goes through my things when I'm down to work.

  Nights I'm playing the desk clerk
at the old Lakeshore Hotel. You know the place.
  We use brand-new bills—
        boy, I'd love a stack of those things!
      They think I'm a widow—otherwise

  no one would give me a chance.
Don, I know I've landed in a real bad spot.
  I've lost twenty pounds
        since skulking back home to Cleveland.
      To think I *wanted* to get thinner!

  Love, Marion

Christmas Trees

How should I now recall
the icy lace of the pane
like a sheet of cellophane,
or the skies of alcohol

poured over the saltbox town?
On that stony New England tableau,
the halo of falling snow
glared like a waxy crown.

Through blue frozen lots
my giant parents strolled,
wrapped tight against the cold
like woolen Argonauts,

searching for that tall
perfection of Scotch pine
from the hundreds laid in line
like the dead at Guadalcanal.

The clapboard village aglow
that starry stark December
I barely now remember,
or the brutish ache of snow

burning my face like quicklime.
Yet one thing was still missing.
I saw my parents kissing,
perhaps for the last time.

Snow

How did we come to this cold place?
It is not listed on the maps.
The cold has disarranged your face.
These memories are not ours, perhaps.

But still we must pretend to know
the reason for things as they are.
We do not recognize the snow.
Perhaps that makes us what we are.

The Servants' Stairs

Always in that back corner,
the paint peeling like burned skin,
and the flight that by some hard twist
brought the pockmarked maid
stumbling into the kitchen,
where we gave our faces to the fire.

IV

Louise Brooks

Certain memories, uncertain,
and bearing toward gentle impoverishment—

Brooks, I mean, of the bow mouth
and ink-rimmed eye, the raccoon's

calculating, injured stare,
and a black coiffure like an Achaean helmet.

There were few like her along the Niobrara.

The End of the Road

Satan stood on the viaduct, suffering laryngitis.
We lived the squalor of the ordinary,

mouth to mouth in those old-school towns
where the dogs still wore collars;

and the preachers, dog collars.
Gold tipped the cattails in the marshes.

A cellophane spread over the fresh pond.
The rusty sores of oaks lingered into spring.

There were other, harsher deadlines,
not that we knew the cost of perfection,

or where to go once we had reached the end.

The Pheasant in His Empires

The fesaunt, skornere of the cok by nyghte.
—Chaucer, *The Parliament of Fowles*

The laser of English sunlight
etches the yellow rape,
heating the stranger's eye
to thoughts of mild escape

to lonely unkempt moors,
the cankered rose of Blake's
benighted chalk-cliffed coasts,
or empty bejeweled lakes.

That steamy summer vision,
bleached in indolence,
admits a single intruder
perched on a wire fence.

Its drenched Tyrrhenian purples,
spit-shined tawny browns,
sharpened glints of silver
trouble the pockmarked downs

that barred the armored legions
breasting the swampy marches
until the border succumbed
to a study of Roman arches.

So civilization was dragged
out of the sunburnt south—
the pin-straight road, lead plumbing,
a bird fit for Caesar's mouth,

and, after the fall of Rome,
belonging in their way
to a place they had once invaded,
the invaders managed to stay.

Dürer's Stag Beetle

Pincers erupt from its skull case,
two Damascene blades
sharpened for some Crusader,
its armor plate enameled in black and brown,

an *à la mode* tailored jacket
just racked by Prada,
though the belly resembles
a computer mouse. Its legs, the spindly legs

of the Paris dancing master,
end in Rorschach blots
or sad India-ink beads,
like broken necklaces of Tahitian pearls.

Ink spot, you are part of your sums,
lowly *Ding an sich*
in that rude philosophy
available only to creatures that crawl.

Not even the most patient bride
would hold such a pose
for more than five hundred years.
Still, who complains about success in design?

O beetle, ever now the hard-
headed bachelor
of the grass-lot realm, never
to know the comforts and solicitations

of the holy marital state
    or the afterlife
    promised to those who worship
the trinity of abdomen, thorax, head,

    bless our belated nuptials,
        delayed past the date
      when wisdom could bow to love
or grace in its grave time, then turn back to stone.

Then, in the Trumpetings

How necessary, meanwhile,
the season of sun-spoilt skies, the rinse

of confirming clouds, even when death
awaits, the next day, the next.

Venice in the Old Days

i

Mist rose from nothing, from the spent idea.
Venice—the last Weberian fantasy,
San Marco isolate, a pawned-off jewel
amid the lowering century's broken lights.
The case was handsome, but the jewel fake.
Women in towering costumes swarmed the noons,
as if our period were an exclamation.
Love is the archive of ordinary time.
Thirty years on, what nags at memory?
Confectioner's snow spilled on ruined cloisters,
a greasy film of water lagging the flagstones
under the dove-gray skies of Italy.
The Roman holidays were not meant for us—
perhaps, in a way, they were not meant at all.

ii

The sunset scraped the gilt dome like a match.
Nothing had lost the kink of purity.
Scrabbling through the beach sand of Murano,
you hauled up dribbling rubies, amethysts.
We stalked reflections of the Risorgimento
through pea-soup mudflats of the drained canal.
The Catholic idea was genocide:
kill everyone—let God sort out the rest.
The phosphorescence on the churches blazed—
no, just limelights touching the numinous.
Two tourists, we lingered nightward, homeward, past
palazzos peeling from their ocher skins.
The vaporetto rocked in acid fog—
what looked like brass to us might have been gold.

The Venetian Dog

Morning drew a damask curtain
across the lagoon. A sketch
would have offered more of the scene,
those hours in Venice, when the powder

tore off the Dolomites, a whitish haze
blinding the edges of the paper.
Weren't we, too, drawn as if
with blunt pencil into the empty margins,

soon to be rubbed clean
with bread crumbs? We stood in the museum
off the Piazza San Marco,
corn snow whipping the glass

as you traced the scribble of a dog,
done two or three centuries past
in a moment of inattention
while the artist sat at coffee

and watched the crowd pass
along the piazzetta—the scrawl
no doubt forgotten,
perhaps consigned to household trash

used by a scullery maid to light the kitchen fire.
Perhaps even the artist himself did not think
the ragged beast worth preserving,
though obviously someone had.

Winter Before Winter

The sky not uniform gray, but a splendor
of chalky washes, some Prussian blue,

smutty or smoky, where stray dots of starlings
whip past like loose punctuation—

the afternoon falters, as afternoons will,
this season of late gestures,

the hardness before true winter.
Botticelli showed the same futility of the beautiful,

caught, held, the merest
stay against the inevitable, the way the first

locust seems a mistake, but soon—
in that way age runs through its petty defeats—

the mobs clatter in the grain bin.
There is that last pleasure, disease.

Winter in Cloud

Canaletto, *Old Walton Bridge over the Thames*

Bean-shaped clouds steal winter's laziness,
the sketch of trees, bare rocks, pale ground below
mare's tails, feathers, the woolen lumps insolvent

and brutish on the swirl of January.
I studied their climbing orders—
only in underpaint could they be stilled.

No wonder I loved the artist's frozen studies,
hovering air on which the smudged and harnessed
    sky
took shape like a dream of smoke, or soot

spooled into drains. In Canaletto's travels,
he found the light of God, the English fire
in cannonading peace dropped

onto a matchstick bridge sawn from ivory.
Beneath the blank sky standing in afterglow,
that heaven would be savior of us all.

On Hair as a Revolutionary Mode of Dress

Each Brutus, each Cato, were none of them fops
But all to a man wore Republican crops.
        —English song of 1794

Our very looks are deciphered into disaffection, and
we cannot move without treading on some political
spring-gun.
        —Coleridge

And so the powder was perforce abandoned
for hair *au naturel*, the gallows look

serving a man as his revealing dress,
the bare neck not necked to the wooden yoke,

though stout informers lingered in doorways,
took ear in every inn, stole a man's letters,

bribed the dull maid who flowered in his kitchen
or the clown who spaded up his dying crop.

Only the fop, the Crown's man, the MP
could pay the guinea tax that Pitt required

on powder, become a *Guinea Pig*, which made
fashion, for once, the badge of loyalty.

A poor man wore his treasons in his hair.
The barber took confession in his shears.

The War

We were the last, the very last, to know.
It was a day like any other day.
Soldiers arrived to take the Jews away.
I saw the neighbor girl with her portmanteau.

What is that thing that people think we owe?
We witnessed scenes more brutal than Doré—
we suffered, too, and sank to our knees to pray.
Someone was first, but we were the last to know.

A Cloudy Sunset in East Anglia

A few glints subtracted the glassine skin
of the crooked pond, like a hand mirror set
on vacant lawns without regret
and so eternally feminine,

the shafts of antique light
not so much the fallen columns of Tyre
but a completeness cast into fire.
We saw that ash could still ignite.

They burned through the plane tree's dowdy dress,
the ordinary days, lively with nothingness.

Night World

The barbed-wire vines
knot the azaleas
in the DMZ

of the border yard.
Everywhere I find
the sign of signs:

the abandoned wreck
of a cardinal's nest,
over-mortgaged,

or underwater;
the snout divots
of armadillos,

shy, unregistered aliens.
The world's another
world at night,

where the dream-scatter
of day lunks about,
preparing, preparing

for nothing at all.

The Troubles

When the householder answered the tentative knock,
he found this scrawny wild-eye of a youth on the step,

ski mask in hand. The boy was dripping—
bangs plastered down, clothes soaked in gasoline,

reeking of the stuff—asking, "Would you be having
a match there, mate? I have need of it."

When the old man shook his head,
the boy said, "Aye. Ta, then."

He turned down the walk, a stream pooling in his
    footsteps.
The teller added, "That boy was a bard, d'you see?

That boy was poetry himself."

On Reading That the Ozone Is in Danger from
Air Conditioning and Amphibious Life
from Shampoo

We, in the day when Earth was burning,
The hour the oceans turned blood red,
Ignored the obvious signs of warning
And took our comforts and are dead.

Head and Shoulders held the sky suspended;
To Frigidaire we preferred to pray;
What God abandoned, Walmart defended,
And lost the world the American way.

There Was

Ohanessian's world-history class,
that grotto of tact
where a millennium of war, disease,
and natural disaster had been shrunk

to the odd fact I could plunder
for exams then murderously forget—
the Tennis Court Oath, Teapot Dome,
Charlemagne, the Diet of Worms,

the Know-Nothings, Aethelred the Unready,
most now by grace forgotten,
until this afternoon's dust-mote-driven air
recalled the Piranesi figure

of the tenth-grade classroom projector
and that washed-out ratchety clip
filmed on the steppes during the Revolution.
A sepia line of men, raggedly dressed,

only their black fleece hats
identifying them as Cossacks,
scruffy, half-starved, shuffled their feet
and, almost as one, leapt back

into a trench we could not see.
Then a second line, a third,
nothing altered but the faces
of bewildered half-boys smiling shyly,

seemingly almost flattered that this act,
their last, was being recorded.
One waggled his fingers in a modest wave.
The hand-cranked camera, the acrobatic

jumps worthy of Keaton, the crack
of bullets in silence: no wonder the clutch
of fifteen-year-olds, in that AP class
of suburban young starters, burst

into raucous laughter.

Lt. Selkirk on the Weymouth

off the coast of Africa

They were not hard to tame, the feral goats.
That rocky mount was hardly an island at all—
I doubt all London is much larger—
and soon the goats and I grew used to our lot.
I had my favorites, or a string of favorites,
because of course the beasts would die,
or break a foreleg, or grow ill-tempered;
and there is nothing like a goat for temper.
But then the kids were so entertaining.
Mary was my darling, dearest Mary.
I would tease her with a parsnip,
or what I named a parsnip—
I'm still not sure what the warty thing was called.

Many was the evening I took her by the fire,
when I had combed for driftwood,
some splinter of spar washed up or, once, two hatches
I used to floor my "house" until the air grew chill.
Mary was my wife those two long years!
She started to cough one afternoon,
and by dawn she was dead.
Oh, how I mourned! I cut my arms
with my dull knife. I cut and cut and let them bleed.

At first I had been neat as a little maid,
for what is a man when he cannot mind himself?
For my business, I squatted behind a mottled dune,
which I called the Dune of Sorrows;
but it's so hard to keep yourself beyond six months—
to keep yourself, I mean, with no one about
to appreciate the daily despair it takes,
not even my precious Mary, whose habits

were slatternly as some Bridewell wench.
I would find her turds in my bed, like love tokens.
I lamed her so she could not stray,
though I was not her only husband, I knew.

Later I lived with Mary's daughter for a time.
She was silky and affectionate,
but I felt a brute. Who could have known
that a grieving man who shat where he stood
would have some compunction
about incest with his goats? And yet I did.

I restored my harem after that. I refused
to take a single wife again, for what use
is the Protestant's marriage when his God
can murder the beloved out of whim?
The goat is a most forgiving Christian—
if you slaughter his mate, if you butcher her
within his sight and roast her over a blazing fire,
why, the next dawn he forgives you!
And yet I felt ashamed. And yet I ate.

I was lord of the cotton tree and palm.
The goats owed fealty to me,
for was I not Alexander the First, Alexander the Good?
Had I not conquered those lands within a week,
and did I not hold the sacred crown,
carved of pimento wood?
A sailor is but a sailor; a king is king forever,
or a little longer, should his subjects be goats.

I clothed myself in my own linens;
but those I owned, those I had drawn from my cabin,
were rags within two seasons.
When my breeches fell away, I dreamed
I was attacked by a native with a spear,

a spear that proved a long iron-nail.
I owned such a nail! And the nail
was soon my needle, and the needle my seamstress,
and my cloth my beloved goats.
When I wanted a new knife, I made the beastly thing
from barrel hoops, for a man may be a blacksmith
if he heats well and hammers hard.
I kept a stolen hammer in my trunk.

What little food I had, I made a banquet—
wild turnips and cabbages decorated
my trencher, seasoned by the pepper berry.
I learned to savor the fish, and fish I caught—
aye, chimney sweepers and old wives,
more fish than the moon could claim.
For meat, there were my dear subjects,
brought to refinement by the salt I dried
from my acres of ocean, my infinite water-fields.
I was a lord of water. Aye, and my realms
bestowed upon me the ten-pound crawfish.
I named each a King William and ate him up.

I never learned to love the taste of rat,
though I knew a mate who believed it
more glorious than English beef
if hung a few days and let grow gamy as mutton.
The bead-eyed beasts used to set upon me
of a night, gnawing at my feet, like cannibals.
I worried the matter for weeks, until I saw
the glow of eyes beyond my spindrift fire. Cats!
More beautiful cats than Dick Whittington knew!
I trained my Praetorian Guard, who labored
for rat, rat raw, rat on the run—
and not once in those long years
did they raise a claw against me.
Nay, I taught my Praetorians to dance!

My other enemies were sea lions, fierce
as those land lions that fright the Afric native.
Mine were fat and made of fat,
stumping along the beach like old sailors.
They tried to crush me like a cake,
not that I possessed a cake.
If I shot one brute, the others would break
into a chorus of such lamentation
I began to fear for my sanity.
When they abandoned that poor soul
to whatever sandy heaven is known to beasts,
I'd have to dig out the ball,
for of powder I had a fair supply;
yet lead was more valuable than gold.
Their delicate oil fatted my lamps.
The meat, if you could call it meat, was sweet and vile.

I read the Bible, for I had not the pen to write
what I might rather read. The Bible
is a hard mistress, and the Bible cannot forgive.
Each day I tore a page to wipe my passage,
beginning with Ecclesiastes.

In short, I converted. I became bishop
of the island congregation of Our Lady of Goats.
The faithful joined in a most liberal fellowship.
I gave communion with a broken bowl and wafers of turnip.
Aye, we believed in Abraham and sacrifice!
We ate whatever appealed to us. We loved
whoever appealed to us. And our God,
our God of Goats, was kind, for He blessed us
with many children. Their bleats
used to keep me awake, beyond the fussing
susurrus of the waves. He was a tolerant God,
the God of Goats, Who never bequeathed us
stone tablets with His laws.

(What is that jest Captain Rogers tells?
Ah, that Moses was the careless man
who broke all ten of the Commandments at once.)
If He had laws, we did not know them.
If He had laws, He did not punish us.
We were to be fruitful and multiply.
And so we were fruitful, and so we multiplied.
I almost was convinced our little daughter
was mine. I knew it could not be so,
though she did favor me about the beard.

When the *Duke*'s sailors rowed ashore,
they were certain I was a goat,
with my goaty hat and goaty beard—
aye, and my goaty head and my goaty eyes.
I was goatishly clad, and my religion was goatish,
down to my goat-bone tools.
One of my knives—I called him the Chopper—
can yet be seen at the Goldenhead, Buckingham Gate,
now pinched with rust, alas.

My frock coat began as the goats', my smallclothes
began as the goats', and whatever was the goats'
was mine—and whatever was mine was the goats'.
All this I could have told the English tars
(I should have said I was gouty,
not goaty); yet, when I made to speak,
all that emerged were squeaks and grunts,
bleats and awful cries. When I had a word,
often I found but half the word, the front or the back,
it hardly mattered. I was reduced
to the cannibal's gesture! The barbarian's index finger!

I should like to be thought a Natural Philosopher,
for I made any number of Surprizing Discoveries—
if only I remembered what they were!

I should have to study myself and scribble it all down.
Of but one thing am I certain, that my goats
thought themselves great controversialists;
and under a pimento tree
we held long philosophic dialogues—
but in whose tongue? The goats', or mine,
or some hideous freak of both? My horned antagonists
were of the Epicurean School—nay, the Rebuttal School!

At last my English returned, and yet what has returned
is never the same. Often now,
when I am rocked in the arms of Morpheus,
I am consoled, not by my dairy maid from Fife,
nor by the Plymouth harridan I chanced to marry,
but by Mary, little Mary, whose eyes were blue,
the blue of the Pacific.

ABOUT THE AUTHOR

William Logan has published ten collections of poetry and six books of essays and reviews. *The Undiscovered Country* won the National Book Critics Circle Award in Criticism. He lives in Gainesville, Florida, and Cambridge, England.

JOHN ASHBERY
Selected Poems
Self-Portrait in a Convex Mirror

PAUL BEATTY
Joker, Joker, Deuce

JOSHUA BENNETT
The Sobbing School

TED BERRIGAN
The Sonnets

LAUREN BERRY
The Lifting Dress

PHILIP BOOTH
Lifelines: Selected Poems 1950–1999

JULIANNE BUCHSBAUM
The Apothecary's Heir

JIM CARROLL
Fear of Dreaming: The Selected Poems
Living at the Movies
Void of Course

ALISON HAWTHORNE DEMING
Genius Loci
Rope
Stairway to Heaven

CARL DENNIS
Another Reason
Callings
New and Selected Poems 1974–2004
Practical Gods
Ranking the Wishes
Unknown Friends

DIANE DI PRIMA
Loba

STUART DISCHELL
Dig Safe

STEPHEN DOBYNS
Velocities: New and Selected Poems: 1966–1992

EDWARD DORN
Way More West

ROGER FANNING
The Middle Ages

ADAM FOULDS
The Broken Word

CARRIE FOUNTAIN
Burn Lake
Instant Winner

AMY GERSTLER
Crown of Weeds
Dearest Creature
Ghost Girl
Medicine
Nerve Storm
Scattered at Sea

EUGENE GLORIA
Drivers at the Short-Time Motel
Hoodlum Birds
My Favorite Warlord

DEBORA GREGER
By Herself
Desert Fathers, Uranium Daughters
God
In Darwin's Room

Men, Women, and Ghosts
Western Art

TERRANCE HAYES
Hip Logic
How to Be Drawn
Lighthead
Wind in a Box

NATHAN HOKS
The Narrow Circle

ROBERT HUNTER
Sentinel and Other Poems

MARY KARR
Viper Rum

JACK KEROUAC
Book of Blues
Book of Haikus
Book of Sketches

JOANNA KLINK
Circadian
Excerpts from a Secret Prophecy
Raptus

JOANNE KYGER
As Ever: Selected Poems

ANN LAUTERBACH
Hum
If in Time: Selected Poems, 1975–2000
On a Stair
Or to Begin Again
Under the Sign

CORINNE LEE
Plenty

PHILLIS LEVIN
May Day
Mercury
Mr. Memory & Other Poems

PATRICIA LOCKWOOD
Motherland Fatherland Homelandsexuals

WILLIAM LOGAN
Macbeth in Venice
Madame X
Rift of Light
Strange Flesh
The Whispering Gallery

ADRIAN MATEJKA
The Big Smoke
Map to the Stars
Mixology

MICHAEL MCCLURE
Huge Dreams: San Francisco and Beat Poems

ROSE MCLARNEY
Its Day Being Gone

DAVID MELTZER
David's Copy: The Selected Poems of David Meltzer

ROBERT MORGAN
Dark Energy
Terroir

CAROL MUSKE-DUKES
An Octave above Thunder
Red Trousseau
Twin Cities

ALICE NOTLEY
Certain Magical Acts
Culture of One
The Descent of Alette
Disobedience
In the Pines
Mysteries of Small Houses

WILLIE PERDOMO
The Essential Hits of Shorty Bon Bon

LIA PURPURA
It Shouldn't Have Been Beautiful

LAWRENCE RAAB
The History of Forgetting
Visible Signs: New and Selected Poems

BARBARA RAS
The Last Skin
One Hidden Stuff

MICHAEL ROBBINS
Alien vs. Predator
The Second Sex

PATTIANN ROGERS
Generations
Holy Heathen Rhapsody
Quickening Fields
Wayfare

SAM SAX
Madness

ROBYN SCHIFF
A Woman of Property

WILLIAM STOBB
Absentia
Nervous Systems

TRYFON TOLIDES
An Almost Pure Empty Walking

SARAH VAP
Viability

ANNE WALDMAN
Gossamurmur
Kill or Cure
Manatee/Humanity
Structure of the World Compared to a Bubble

JAMES WELCH
Riding the Earthboy 40

PHILIP WHALEN
Overtime: Selected Poems

ROBERT WRIGLEY
Anatomy of Melancholy and Other Poems
Beautiful Country
Box
Earthly Meditations: New and Selected Poems
Lives of the Animals
Reign of Snakes

MARK YAKICH
The Importance of Peeling Potatoes in Ukraine
Unrelated Individuals Forming a Group Waiting to Cross